GROWING UP WHITE

GROWING UP WHITE

An Oreo's Guide to Fitting In

Kevin L. White

BROWNIE FOX
Publishing Company

BROWNIEFOX PUBLISHING LLC, 2019

Published by Browniefox Publishing, Huber

Heights, Ohio. Library of Congress Cataloged

First Printing: 2019

Second Edition: 2020

Illustrations by James Fields IV

ISBN 978-1-7332726-2-9 paperback

Request for information may be sent to the

following address: Browniefox Publishing LLC
6827 Charlesgate Rd
Huber Heights, Ohio, 45424

www.browniefoxpublishing.com

U.S. trade bookstores and wholesalers: Please contact Browniefox

Publishing LLC Tel: 9376232629

Browniefoxpublishing@gmail.com

Dedication

To my late father who taught me how to be an independent thinker.

Contents

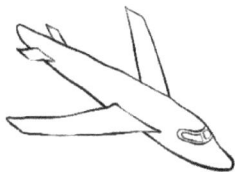

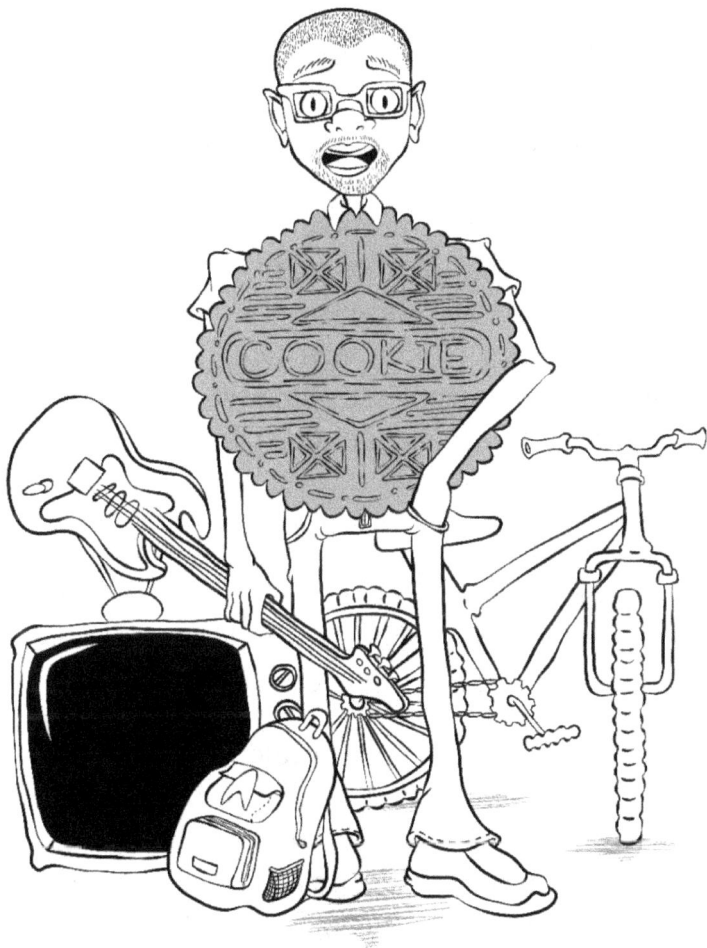

Preface

The purpose of this book is to highlight and make fun of a social issue very close to me and many others who have been called Oreos solely based on the way we act or don't act. Although Oreo isn't always a positive identity to live with in many communities, there are those who wear the label with pride, and some even have YouTube videos and web pages touting their Oreo lives. Others are unhappy, even depressed about their status because they feel isolated and ultimately blame their parents for their condition.

An Oreo life can be burdensome at times, but in key situations it can be advantageous. This book as a guide gives insight into different aspects of situations and problems that may arise in Oreo culture.

The goal of this book is twofold: to bring awareness to Oreo culture and to explain its impact in both Black and White cultures. I hope the information contained in the following chapters will help ease the anxiety many Oreos living in this great and diverse country experience.

The terms "Blacks" and "Whites," as I use them, don't pertain to everyone, nor do they apply to every situation. In this book you will hopefully find insight through personal observations, as flawed as they may seem. I hope you enjoy reading this book as much as I did writing it.

Thank you.

Introduction

My name is Kevin. I am an African American, or so they say. I have been to Africa, but I don't see any reason to call myself African American; that is just a label they put on people who only appear to be Black. I am also of Italian and English heritage, based on my DNA makeup, but nobody seems to care about my other identities; to the outside world, my skin color is dark, so I am labeled African American. When filling out forms, I am forced to check the African American box on every document. If you have thick lips, nappy hair, and darker than average skin, welcome to the club, brothers and sisters. Isn't that how we are referred to? It's not that I'm not proud of my African American heritage, I just don't like to be put in that stereotypical race box that strips me of my individuality. There have been times when I've checked the Other Race box on applications just for fun, to mess with the people reading it. Are we being classified and cataloged? Does it matter what I look like? Is our society so shallow that we must categorize each other by sight?

The title *Growing Up White* has a double meaning—it refers to growing up in a predominately White society, AND it's a play on words. Are you ready for it? My last name is White! How ironic!

From childhood through adulthood, many events have shaped the way I think and act today, which I would say is more in line with White culture than Black. As is believed of Whites, I think analytically, I have no rhythm, I like mayonnaise, and I adore Barry Manilow. I believe myself to be the ultimate Oreo, right? I should credit the movie *Undercover Brother* for the mayo reference. I had no idea that was a stereotype until I watched it. What's up with the hot sauce anyway? I would never put hot sauce on anything! NEEEEVER!

Before I go any further, let me clarify what I mean when I use the terms Black, White, and Real Black People, identified throughout this book simply as RBP. Then I will get into the discussion of what exactly an Oreo is, other than a sandwich cookie! Black, White, and RBP are identifiers that lead to stereotypical expectations from others. The terms Black and White, when referring to people, are an integral component of the stratification of society and have given rise to many prejudices, biases, and assumptions.

The term Real Black People (RBP) is mine, and it is my way, however feeble, to identify that part of the African

American community that totally identifies with Black culture. My intent is in no way an attempt to cast aspersions upon these individuals.

According to *Wikipedia.com,* "An Oreo is a sandwich cookie consisting of two chocolate disks with a sweet cream filling in between. The version currently sold in the USA is made by Nabisco. Oreo has become the best-selling cookie in the United States since its introduction in 1912." Now, according to the *Urban Dictionary,* "An Oreo is what a Black person gets called if they appear to be "Black" on the outside but act like they are "White" on the inside."

Other slang terms applied to us include "coconuts," "cornball brothers," "House Negroes," "Uncle Toms," and other creative terms. These terms are offensive to some and a badge of honor to others. I have been called every one of these by Blacks but never by Whites. Even to this day I am singled out by Real Black People (RBP) as not being Black enough, while to White People I am Black because my skin is dark. Consequently, I end up not "fitting in" anywhere, and this leads me to feel socially disadvantaged. What is a real Black person? Someone with qualifying skin colors? How am I supposed to act?

We Oreos may live a "quite White" lifestyle, but we naturally like the bass turned up for even our geekiest of songs. Now, I am not saying my White brothers and sisters don't like bass and prefer treble, but maybe Oreos and other Blacks like it just a bit more? In my opinion, there is nothing worse than being in someone's ride where the bass is not appreciated. We may even surreptitiously jack up the bottom when the driver is not looking! They make that EQ for reason. Maybe you don't think it's a genetic thing to enjoy bass, but I believe it to be true.

If you are an Oreo and your exposure to Black culture has been extremely limited, it can have an enormous impact on your social identity. Believing the convenient lie that you somehow really are a White person in dark skin comes with its own unique problems. After years of disappointment, and after reflecting on how I ever thought such a flawed philosophy was a reasonable idea, I eventually came to realize the ridiculousness of it all. I have to say, though, ignorance is bliss when you have no clue. Unlike the frog in the proverbial boiling pot, I eventually recognized the pitfalls of my euphoric ignorance.

Being an Oreo isn't easy, especially when you can't fake your skin color (unless of course, you take drastic measures with skin bleaching, plastic surgery, etc.). Being black-skinned means you are supposed to have the natural Black lingo down. If you don't, do not attempt to talk "Black" in public because it will never sound good enough; not now, not next week, not next year, not EVER. Even if you practice in front of your full-length mirror day-in and day-out, it's not going to happen. Just sayin'. What may sound good and passable to you will be your undoing with those who really are down for the cause. You may be able to fool your White friends, but those who are Blacker than you will call you out and embarrass you. The more I tried to be Black, the more obvious it was that I was merely a pretender, or should I say I was trying to "front." Is that the term? There should be Black-acting survival classes for us Oreos; that class would be worth at least 3 credit hours. The classes would need to be staffed with RBP citizens, of course.

Reality Check

The following scene was my first taste of racial inequality between Blacks and Whites in my early life. Yes, there were occasional name-calling episodes in the Deep South when we went off base, but as a sheltered military dependent, I never took them seriously. I looked at these instances as isolated events from people I didn't have daily contact with. Besides, racial slurs, inequality, and related negative language was forbidden in military neighborhoods and schools. If you used such language or actions, the parent who was in the military had to answer to his commander about it. I know you're falling asleep hearing about my childhood, but the main point is that we all got along.

When I was a bright-eyed, bushy-tailed, Afro-sporting young man growing up off base in Virginia, I enjoyed my school mates, neighborhood friends, and the incredible diversity of people that were literally from every corner of the world. We truly appreciated the different cultures that surrounded us

Back in the '70s, we had nothing better to do than play outside every chance we got. We only had one American channel on TV and one American station on the radio, so there are gaps in television shows and radio songs I never heard in that time period that I am not familiar with even today. From early in the morning after breakfast, catching lunch, and scarfing down dinner, we truly were children of the neighborhood. We were tight-knit with each other and we never had negative issues or divisions of race that I can remember. We were all individuals who saw the contrary as silly and dismissed them as they came. Being sheltered is a two-edged sword, and we were holding the wrong end of it.

The older we got, the more apparent it was that some of the parents from the 1950s era were not as accepting as their own children. My father, having grown up in the real world, always gave me advice I thought I had no need to heed. One day he asked me if I noticed if my White friends preferred to talk to their other White friends over me. I was very puzzled! I thought, why would he say that? All my friends were no different than I! We were all the same, were we not? Years later, reality hit me when I noticed I was being treated differently after school was over. If I did go to some of my friends' houses, the parents didn't exactly greet me with open arms.

When we lived off base in Virginia, I was once threatened by a motorhead father working on his car that I would be punished if I came too close to him when he was working. I remember he was waving a wrench at me when he said it. I had no idea what he was talking about at the time, but the words stuck with me for life. Essentially, he was saying, "Stay away son, you aren't welcome here." I'm not saying they were racist at all. I would say maybe they were just like me with their identity ideals, and they saw me as I saw other Blacks I was indifferent to. For the most part, military brats see their friends as just friends regardless of race. Yes, we knew we were different colors and religions, but we respected each other as individuals and celebrated our uniqueness.

When my father retired from the military in 1980, we moved from Spring Lake, North Carolina, to Columbus, Ohio. Going from military DOD schools to a public-school district, I discovered an odd thing: Blacks and Whites didn't live in the same neighborhoods. We moved into a rental on the far east side of town in a neighborhood about a mile or two from Walnut Ridge High School. I had been called an Oreo ever since my Father retired from the United States Air Force, and we were forced to live in what we thought were the mean streets of suburban Columbus, Ohio. Being a military brat, I was completely insulated from the perceived differences between Whites and Blacks outside of the military life.

The neighbors were completely different than what I was used to in military housing. They weren't as supportive; in fact, they were suspicious of our motives for some reason. I remember my sister Jana being put on a bus to Johnson Park Middle School, which was located halfway to the Black neighborhoods, for what I thought was a social nightmare! On the bus, three of the Black kids were sitting in the back trying to force the White kids, who were already in the back, to give up their seats and move to the front. What?! Strangely, the White kids were submissive to the rowdy Blacks that pushed them around. I wondered why they never fought back. I thought we were all equal. What the heck was going on here? My White friends would never put up with that!

Day one at Johnson Park was traumatizing! The school was about 70% Black and 30% White. Sounds good, right? Not so much! Don't get me wrong, there were Blacks that I was friends with on the bases I had lived on, but they just weren't of the same cultural background. I could not identify with them; their culture and behavior were foreign to me. I witnessed Black male students who, to me, seemed overly aggressive, and who would taunt random White male students. On more than one occasion, two Black males would literally football tackle White males on the grass outside during lunch period. When would I be their next victim of their game? What kind of alien planet was I on? Why didn't the White kids fight back? None of this made sense to me.

Meanwhile, I was worried about my older sister Jana, who was having troubles of her own fitting in. Besides being bullied for the way she walked, she wore a perm to school once and was ridiculed for "trying to be White."

Jana and I went home from the first day of school and begged Dad to move us to a different school system because we didn't like the kids at Johnson Park. We were terrified!! I don't want to stereotype everyone as acting the same, but as I've heard somewhere before, one rotten apple can spoil the bunch. In this case it seemed as if the whole cart was spoiled.

Things slowly got easier as the school year went on; we figured out the right people to hang with and what areas to avoid. I never sat near the back of the bus again; I considered it too risky to take chances with. As for lunch time, I stayed inside the cafeteria where it was safer.

The good news is that my sister and I were able to dive into other avenues in school; mine was music and hers was art. In those domains, we found our escape and made friends with others, both Black and White. We all had common interests, and I was very happy with that, but I felt that I could never truly develop the deep friendships I had before; our worlds were drastically different. My sister became an art major and I continued feeding my passion in the world of music. We we're clinging to our artistic comforts, which we need- ed more than we realized at the time. All my friends in high school were in the music program. Not surprising, huh?

Oreo-ethos

According to the *Oxford Dictionary,* the definition of ethos is "the characteristic spirit of a culture, era, or community as manifested in its beliefs and aspirations." The ethos of Oreos is one of inclusion, respect, and tolerance. To use the Oreo cookie as an analogy, we can enjoy both aspects equally. An Oreo has a dark, chocolate cookie that lives in harmony with the sweet, creamy filling in the middle. To apply this to life, others are often not so tolerant of the Oreo trying to indulge in both sides of White and Black culture; we get the message loud and clear that we are to choose one only. We do not want to be forced to choose, as we enjoy many aspects of both elements. Why wouldn't we, since we were raised in both? Yet we are told by RBP's to shun all things White. This creates a dilemma!

There are two separate worlds in which all Oreos live. I invite you to join me in calling it the Oreo ethos, or the "Ore-ethos." Like an Oreo cookie, caught between the Black, dark, and delicious cookie and the sweet, White cream filling, it's really the best of both worlds in that we can indulge and enjoy each part of the cookie equally. Or can we? We are, of course, Black on the outside and, well, you know, mentally White on the inside.

While interacting with the White world, Oreos appear to enjoy a hunky-dory existence. They identify much more with the White community they were raised in. In their tenuous minds, they think they're just another White-like neighbor, fully acceptable, and part of the larger good of their communities.

Acceptance of Oreos is widespread in their world, or so they believe with all their heart. Oreos are considered safe in the White world because they never display the stereotype actions associated with RBP's (Real Black People). Together, Oreos and Whites all get along... until certain lines are crossed that cause people to reject them, only to be lumped in with RBP's.

What lines do Oreos make the mistake of crossing? We won't even get into dating issues, especially back in my day. Well, maybe just a little bit needs to be said here. Really, it's important. Although today it's much more acceptable to date outside one's race, it's still somewhat of a line some people don't want to cross without weighing the costs.

Some people don't care how White the Oreo may act, he or she is just another Black person to them. *Guess Who's Coming to Dinner* doesn't play on every TV set in some homes! When it came to interracial dating in my days, when parents forbade such things in my community, it was more like *Nightmare on Elm Street*. In my early years, living off-base, it was a huge deal. Now it's very commonplace, which is a great thing. But that's another book, so let's not go there, okay?

The Oreo Dilemma

*The Oreo dilemma is the suppression of any stereo-
typical Black behaviors or activities that would com-
promise your Oreo status as an acceptable equal to a
White person.*

My lifestyle does not fit in with the Black "cause," a cause which I have never professed to be a part of or understood. But we will get into that later. I LIKE my status as an acceptable equal in the White world. I try very hard to maintain that hard-earned acceptance by avoiding behavior that is stereotypically identified as "Black."

One example of that stereotype focuses on food. We know that food is often a strong identifier of one's culture. Consider watermelon, my most favorite food of all time. Well, you probably know where I am going with this! I cannot indulge in this delicious, sweet, juicy, fruit in front of my White friends for fear that I will prove the stereotype that Blacks love watermelon! Oh, and some side joke as to how far I can spit the seeds! Meanwhile, my White friends can enjoy watermelon in their front yards, that juicy sweetness running down their arms, to their hearts' content with nary a care. It is not fair! Gosh, how I would love to join them but, NO!

And, get this! If I am looking at watermelons in the grocery store, sometimes people come up to me to ask for advice as to which is the "best" melon. Well, heck, I don't know! Yet, I am considered the watermelon authority based on my skin color. This is crazy! The truth is, I probably am the last person one should ask because if I ever DO buy a watermelon at the store, I just grab one and get it in my cart as fast as I can. Really, I would rather be asked to help someone get an item off a tall shelf, as my height, 6'2", gives me that "reach" advantage. Now, you are probably thinking I am overly sensitive to this watermelon thing, and you would be wrong. It has happened too many times to be mere coincidence.

Another food I absolutely love is chicken: fried, county fried, Kentucky fried, baked, BBQed, boiled, grilled, Cajun blackened, or broiled. If it is chicken, I'm probably going to like it. Eating chicken outside of the privacy of our own homes sets us up for ridicule and judgment just as does watermelon, even among those who we consider friends. I absolutely refuse to take chicken to the workplace for lunch, especially fried, as I more than likely will be asked where the watermelon is. No, seriously! So, Oreos, here's a tip: When ordering food for lunch, it is okay to order the chicken sandwich from a non-chicken restaurant, but never, ever bring in a bucket of chicken from anywhere! If you do, it's all over, and there go the sirens! I REALLY would like to be able to just eat my chicken in peace!

IF, and this is a big if, IF I EVER take chicken into work, it will be disguised in one of those ubiquitous storage containers and mixed with innocuous foods such as rice and veggies. There you go, chicken incognito! Plastic containers are like the privacy fence, designed to keep certain things or people in and certain things or people out! People feel like they are invading your privacy if they breach the fence barrier, so they don't look inside your protected lunch. Open plates, however, are fair game; they are not protected under the "Container Privacy Act of 2019!" It IS possible to have a security breach, so it is worth being extra careful. Microwave it and (sniff, sniff), "Is that CHICKEN I smell?"

Eating in my car is another option, but that can be problematic if, again, there is a lingering odor, OR, God forbid! I leave traces of evidence, such as tiny grease spots on my shirt! It is generally safe to take the side dishes into work, no questions asked. The secret to this food issue is to show no rinds or bones that can be seen or traced to you. If they do find them, you know who they are going to pin it on, right? The Black person!

I must confess, though, that I HAVE had some fun playing with these stereotypes. Sometimes, if I'm in the mood, I will accept the taunting and I let the stereotype play out all the way. This is the point where us Oreos will slip into the Black identity full bore and behave in the ways expected of us. Sometimes it's kind of fun to jerk people's chains that way.

There was the time in Air Force technical training that I bought a flat box of chicken from KFC. I had it out on the eating table in my dorm room, so a few of my friends who stopped by saw it and made their own snide comments about it. What did I do? The next week I played on the stereotype and threw a chicken and watermelon party for a few of my close friends! I got a whole bucket of KFC and a whole watermelon that we had to cut open with a guitar string because the mess kitchen was closed.

Those were good times, but looking back, I'm not sure my behavior was okay, even though I was with close friends. I thought I was poking fun at the stereotypes, but could it be that I just encouraged the propagation of them? I thought I was heightening Black stereotype awareness, but was I, or had I just become a cheap imitation of an RBP? To this day, I can't answer my own question, but one thing I do know is that we Oreos often feel betwixt and between within the Oreo dilemma: Which culture is going to be the focus of our energy for acceptance today? Either direction in the name of socialization can be a mixed bag—sometimes we are comfortable enough striving for acceptance, but other times we've just had enough and really don't want to deal with the whole role-playing thing.

So the battle rages on. Too often, when we try to interact within the Black community, it just does not work and we are accused of being fakes, of parading in disguise. We are hassled about acting White, talking the way White people do, and not supporting Black values. There is disdain, hatred, and resentment in the tone that is used. According to many RBP's, Oreos are an inferior version of the Black person and don't deserve to be acting Black. The truth is, we are not acting at all, we are simply living the life that we learned from the culture in which we were raised, which was predominantly White. That's it! There are no hidden agendas, and we certainly don't feel superior in any way. We WANT to be accepted within the community, and we want to band together with our brothers and sisters in denouncing racism and discrimination. Oreos suffer the same racism same as real Blacks do. Oreos have their own unique stereotypes they live with. All of them come from "real" Black people.

The ironic thing, though, is that RBP's engage in these very behaviors, but rather than having an attitude of acceptance and inclusion, they exclude us because they believe us to be disingenuous and, as I said, not down for the cause. On the flip side, the culture where we feel most comfortable is filled, too, with people who don't understand us. There's a myriad of assumptions about us that is strictly based on our skin color. Assumptions such as what we like to eat, how we vote, how we like to entertain, where we live (or should live), and with whom we like to hang. Since we are black-skinned, it is assumed that we are experts in all things Black, including what's up in the hood. Heck, we don't know! But if we profess this, we are likely to get incredulous looks, as if to say, "Well, you're Black, how is it that you don't know?" I'm not saying all White people think like this, but enough do. Us Oreos try hard to act in ways that refute assumptions, that prove we are "safe." We insist, "No, we are not Black like that!" In fact, most Blacks are not "Black like that."

Because our motives are those of harmony and inclusion, and because our behavior models this type of thinking, we hope that we aren't being judged, at least when we are moving in our comfort zone. We hope to prove that the assumptions are incorrect. But hey, who are we kidding? An Oreo can't win, no matter how hard he or she tries. The question is, when will the insanity stop?! When can we coexist as equals, human being to human being, and not be viewed as adversaries?

As should be obvious, being raised in a White world is the seed that blossoms into the development of the Oreo dilemma. It reminds me of the story of the boy who was raised by wolves. The boy does not know that he really is NOT a wolf until he has experiences in the non-wolf world. It is then that his wolf ways are considered wrong, deviant, if you will. The boy learns that he really is not a wolf, yet he is not wanting or willing to abandon his wolf ways or his "pack." Why do others create of this dilemma, this idea that a choice needs to be made as to which direction to go? Same goes for us Oreos.

We KNOW we aren't White. We understand our physical reality, and we also understand our social and mental state, which makes us comfortable with White culture. We don't like being put in the position of needing to choose one over the other, and truth be told, as previously discussed, either choice we make is the wrong one. The boy raised as a wolf can't win, and Oreos can't win either because we don't "fit" and can't fit due to the way we were raised.

A lot of this nonsense would be a non-issue if it weren't for class stratification and the perceptions that result from this stratification. It is stratification (to be discussed later) that creates the environment where Whites are more comfortable with other Whites of the same social and economic class, and the same is true for Blacks. As in the wolf analogy, were all seem most comfortable running with our "pack." For the Oreo, it is a bit more complicated because of the Oreo dilemma: "With which group should I try to run today, my White com-patriots or my Black brothers and sisters? Who is going to be more receptive?"

The chicken and watermelon examples are stereotypi-cal racial manifestations I never thought about before we transitioned into the unsheltered real world. My race-consciousness levels were raised as a result of these negative experiences.

The next year, we moved to an almost all-White neigh-borhood a block away from the high school. After the experiences at Johnson Park Middle School, I soon real-ized that many of the Whites in my new neighborhood thought we were no different than the RBP's. For the first time in my life, I found I had to prove my Oreo status to people that didn't know me. The stark reality was that I became an RBP to everyone that did not know me as an individual. It was scary because I knew exactly how and why they did; I felt the exact same way about other RBP's I didn't know.

In high school, I found solace as a band geek, where there were people that shared my interest in music. The year I attended Walnut Ridge was the year they intro-duced bussing to our school, and many Blacks from other parts of the city started attending. There were ri-ots and protests during that year; race relations were very strained. Outside of band I was a fish out of water.

I avoided the Black students, who I felt uncomfortable with. But I was okay once I got to know people, and things started to smooth out my freshman year when I started playing football. Other Blacks I didn't know well enough were avoided based on behavior. Looking back, I regret not being equipped enough to overcome in those days.

The Power of Perceptions and Assumptions

O reos, as much as most people, want to be perceived as acceptable and safe, so we are very careful not to display the stereotypical behavior associated with RBP. We tend to believe that we get along with Whites and that we are viewed more as equals than not, but the reality is that this is just an illusion. Oh sure, things seem hunky-dory until… Once we cross certain lines, we are viewed the same way RBP's are, and that category is one of unacceptability to many in the White community.

What lines do Oreos make the mistake of crossing, you ask? Dating Whites, eating the wrong foods in public, moving into an all-White neighborhood, visiting a small town where there are no Blacks, along with others I'll mention later in this book.

Unfortunately, we, as human beings, tend to perceive differences and create barriers based on what our eyes alone can see. If it's not color of skin, it's height, weight, the kind of clothes worn, etc. Additionally, many people use their status as a guide to how to relate to other human beings. These identifiers create class stratifications and are applied particularly to people we don't know. For example, when I was in Air Force technical school, I made friends with a guy I met from Illinois, who I only saw in uniform for the first four weeks. When we got the freedom to wear street clothes, I was amazed that this guy, who I thought I knew, was wearing biker gear! Immediately I categorized him, and thought I knew how I should interact with him based on my judgment of what I believed about all "biker dudes." That's a shame on me for thinking that way. He was still the same person, but now I had put a barrier between us, wrecking the friendship we had developed, all because of appearances.

The same thing happens with skin color, even moreso, perhaps, due to the saliency of this identifier. All my friend had to do was superficially change his appearance and I judged him according to how I was "programmed" by society to judge him. Regarding skin color, there are no superficial changes that can be made. For me and other fellow Oreos, this is particularly problematic as our skin color shouts Black, i.e., DANGEROUS! But the Oreo ethos is opposite of dangerous. The Oreo spirit is one of embracement, empowerment, of promoting acceptance of differences, a sense of comradery, and a mindset of "we're all in this together."

Stratification

S tratification of races creates a conflicting dynamic that can make an Oreo skittish, as RBP's don't understand our ethos (again, we are viewed as "sell-outs" to them), and Whites don't get it either. As can be said for many, only our true friends "get it" and, as is often the case with Whites, the whole stratification thing is not so forefront in their minds.

For the Oreo, stratification is particularly problematic because one huge identifier in the stratification paradigm, skin color, drives people to make assumptions about what the Oreo is like. Because our skin color is "Black," we must be... (whatever thoughts, ideas, and behaviors mainstream society somehow attributes to ALL Black people). Whites have this great advantage in that individualism is much more acknowledged; part of the White ethos is an understanding of diversity within the population.

It is exhausting being an Oreo as we are constantly looking for others to gain an understanding of how they should relate to us. There is no stratification category for Oreos, so we are put in the Black category based on the visual: what can be seen. I sense that you might like an example.

Todd is a professional Oreo who lives in the suburbs, where there are few homes in which a Black person resides. Yes, this generally means this is a suburban neighborhood, and it is the only kind of neighborhood in which Todd has ever lived. Todd is well known, and when his neighbor is asked to describe him, this is what he says:

Identifier #1: Todd is a Black man.
Identifier #2: Todd is articulate.
Identifier #3: Todd is an insurance underwriter.

Now, Todd uses identifiers as well, but notice the huge differences:

Identifier #1: Mr. Schmidt is a marketing executive.
Identifier #2: Mr. Schmidt drives a Mercedes.
Identifier #3: Mr. Schmidt is a swell guy.

As you can see, Todd is immediately identified as being Black—that is his FIRST and most salient characteristic, and that is the box in which he is put. There is no such box for Mr. Schmidt, who is addressed by a more respectful title, in case you missed that! The Black identifier must mean that Todd likes rap music, enjoys chitterlings, fried chicken, etc.

Nothing is wrong with any of these things if they aren't considered to be hard and fast characteristics of Todd and his individuality is ignored. Todd might be surprised to know that his skin color was STILL the first thing mentioned, even though everyone on his street knows him well, because he evaluates everyone using a different measure.

Todd believes to be among his "own kind," as this is the only environment he has ever known. His neighborhood is the one place where he feels safe and accepted. His neighborhood is his "sanctuary," away from the injustices of the world, and a place where he is comfortable with his social situation. It is when Oreos leave their White comfort zone that consists of family and friends that the social ethos is perceived as being much more precarious. Todd might be surprised that a question that his neighbors entertain, thought but unvoiced, is, "What are the reasons Todd chooses to live here rather than with people who share more things in common with him?" Um, the "common" being skin color, of course. That question: Why is the person not living in "the hood"?

Todd represents the epitome of the Oreo ethos AND the Oreo dilemma. Todd truly holds dear his White cultural values, yet getting ahead works differently for him than what he has been taught. Others view him based on his Black appearance. As my late father told me more than once, "We must work harder than everyone else to move ahead in life."

Say Todd has worked hard and performed well on the job, but is still passed over for a promotion. His dilemma is this: "Did I get passed over due to my "identity" as Black, or is there truly something upon which I need to improve?" There's the rub, the dilemma, and even if he were to ask why he did not get the promotion, and it WAS due to his identity as a Black man, he will not be told straight up; that element would be denied because THAT is discrimination. Does discrimination happen anymore? Ha! You know it does!

Oreos often don't feel they belong anywhere. Since there is no stratification level identified as "Oreo," there are no reference points, nothing to help people understand our ethos. Therefore, we are outcasts, doing our best to survive in an environment where our behaviors often make us targets.

Consider the former "military brat" and Washington Redskins quarterback RGIII. In 2012, he amassed 3,200 yards for passing, 20 TD's (touchdowns), and 815 yards rushing—as a rookie! He was a great contribution to the NFL, and became a hero to many Black youth. However, he was about to break culture and marry a White woman, Rebecca Liddicoat. THAT became the focus of ESPN Black columnist Robert Parker. According to Parker, RGIII was not "down for the cause." I would really like to have a discussion with Parker and ask him just what he meant by that statement. I think I have some idea, as that very same comment was made to me not long ago. It implies that we have turned our back on the "brotherhood," so in the minds of people like Robert Parker, RGIII, myself, and other Oreos like us are not "Black enough." Parker went so far as to apply a derogatory term towards RGIII, one I mentioned earlier: Cornball brother. According to the *Urban Dictionary,* the definition of cornball brother is: "A man of Black/African American descent who does not support, nor does he identify with the Black/African American community."

Nobody ever goes after Robin Thicke or Justin Timberlake for not being White enough. Maybe we should call out Michael Vick for being too Black. How come nobody has gone after quarterback Tom Brady for being too White? That ain't going to happen because it seems like only Black people care about other Blacks being Black enough. People love Whites who sing like Blacks!

You'll rarely see Black people break into country, rock, or bluegrass music. No one expects that to happen or wants to see it. But Oreos have the background and ability to make those genres viable based on their cultural backgrounds.

Sellout

The Oreo's natural enemy, if you will, is the Black community, the very community where you would think a person of the same color would be embraced. But NO! Blacks are not tolerant of people who look like them but don't act as they do. At first glance, an Oreo may not be "outed," but once the Oreo opens his or her mouth, he or she will probably give him or herself away and thus be judged as not authentically Black. Criticizing Oreos seems to be an unwritten rule that many Blacks enjoy. Oreo discrimination is real, and it is very upsetting—Oreos would like to be respected as part of the Black community.

Trying to understand why RBP's (Real Black People) don't like Oreos is a mystery to me. What I do know is if you become successful and benefit financially, or if you choose to move into a more exclusive neighborhood, you will be branded as a "sell-out" or as trying to act White. The fact of the matter is, in most cities the neighborhoods "sell-outs" move to are generally populated with White people. The Black person moving into such a neighborhood is doing so for the reason everyone else is: It's a nice neighborhood with good schools, more conveniences, and less crime. The racial make-up should not be a factor, but it becomes an issue. Are the only people who can purchase the 5,000-square foot home with the granite countertop kitchen and in-ground pool without fear of being labeled a "sell-out" Whites? Why is "moving up" considered a sell-out? A Black person moving up does not indicate that that person has abandoned his or her roots; it has more to do with lack of economic advantage and opportunity in the inner-city environment. It means not having to drive out of one's way to shop for one's wants and needs. It should be all good, yet, alas, taking advantage of the things that more prosperous communities have to offer is looked down upon by many RBP's. This is a reality across the U.S.A. Cities like Trotwood, Ohio, which most department stores and restaurants have left due to economic downfall, have been losing their residents as well to nearby cities that have better opportunities and services.

Is this same dynamic true in White culture? I think not! Whites don't seem to care if a successful neighbor moves to a more prosperous neighborhood. They aren't labeled as "sell-outs." More likely, they are congratulated and asked all about their new home. Heck, there often is even a housewarming party, either hosted by the new owners or by one of their friends! No one questions why they made the choice to move; it's understood and accepted that the person has a right to better his or her existence. Again, I say, "Stop the insanity!" In my opinion, selling out should be everyone's goal. We are all chasing the "American Dream," to move above and beyond one's present circumstances. All of this requires ambition—something to be admired, not scorned. The covert rule for Blacks stemming from the Black community itself seems to be "stick with your own kind."

This business of selling out permeates the life of an Oreo; I could write a separate book on this topic alone! At this time, though, I am going to highlight two other areas where us Oreos can get slammed by RBP's.

Politics: We Blacks are kind of expected to all vote the same for every issue and candidate. During election season, you hear all about the "Black vote" and which candidate or which issue is going to appeal more to the "Black vote." If a Black person votes differently from the expected "Black vote," that person becomes a sellout; again, not down for the "cause." But us Oreos are often more in tune with White culture, so what does "the Black vote" mean to us? If one of us Oreos was the only black-skinned person interviewed at an exit poll and shared our White-leaning bent, would we be considered a statistical outlier, or would the media portray us as the "voice" of the Black community? If portrayed as the "voice," then there is the assumption that we voted along color lines and that we are all one homogeneous group, devoid of any independent thinking abilities. But to the Black community, we expose ourselves as traitors. Does this happen to White people? I think not! I may stand corrected, but I don't believe there is any such term as "the White vote." What, Whites think independently and us Blacks don't? How absurd!

Those whose cast is predominantly Black often have as the focus the idea of being a "sell-out," of abandoning one's roots for the purpose of gaining money or fame. *The Fresh Prince of Bel-Air* TV series was, in my view, essentially a depiction of Oreos vs. RBP's. The Oreo Banks family were successful, wealthy and acted "White."

They were portrayed as bougie sell-outs who had abandoned their roots. Meanwhile, Will, a "down" Black teen from the heart of West Philadelphia, never lost his roots, so his character was given the moral license to call out Carlton for selling out and acting too White. Some scripts called for Mr. and Mrs. Banks to realize how wrong it was to forget their roots, and repent for their mistaken ways, apologizing and salvaging their dignity.

The Banks family often looked like fools as the cool-handed Will always kept them aware of RBP parameters. The Fresh Prince's faithful "down for the cause" partner, D.J. Jazzy Jeff, helped him take the Bankses down another level when deemed necessary. The *Fresh Prince* series represented the audacity of success to the Black community. The message of the show was to make fun of people who act White and have turned against their Black roots, or at least this is the way I view the narrative.

Ask or AKS?

One thing that sets us Uncle Tom, cornball Oreos apart and gives us away is the language we use. People don't expect us to talk "White" because Black skin equals Black talk. Oreos pronounce their R's correctly and use proper grammar when conveying ideas to their friends. We use the word ask not the tool word that's supposed to be employed to cut down trees. Axe? "Pardon me but you want to axe what?"

Oreos, when we try to throw down with our Black counterparts, don't always say or wear the right things. We still pronounce our R's and refrain from using the word aks! You'll never hear us say things like, "Lemme aks you something, homey." Trying to throw down with the Black language will make you sound like a fool if you don't practice it or live it every day. After all, you can't teach an old dog (dawg) new tricks. Word to the wise, my fellow Oreo brothers and sisters: stop tryna front on the real deal. "You down?" We won't even go into handshakes. Ugh, jeepers!

Oreos are considered safe to Whites because they never display the stereotypical actions usually associated with RBP's (Real Black People). They all get along un-til certain lines are crossed that cause people to reject Oreos and subsequently lump them in with RBP's. I have an old Black friend in Columbus named Jay. We used to be in an Oreo-friendly jazz band as a hobby. We only had one gig, but that's neither here nor there. He played sax, and I played the second of two trumpets. One night we were hanging out with some of our mu-sician friends, cruising through the streets of Colum-bus, when Jay yelled out a "ghetto"-inspired phrase. Immediately our Keyboardist remarked, "Wow, Jay, you sounded like a real Black person." There you go! Jay just blew our cover!

The keyboardist had all along accepted us as safe Blacks, even though I never thought he thought of us that way. To this day, it still bothers me. The funny thing is, Jay isn't even an Oreo! He behaved like one but didn't grow up that way. I'm puzzled, though, how the keyboardist figured out we weren't down for the "cause." I thought I had him convinced, and then Boom! The cat was out of the bag. Where did I go wrong?

Where did Jay and I go wrong? We intentionally acted Black in front of him. We must have overdone it to the point we sounded phony to him. By the way, because Jay was Oreo-like, we were the best of friends in high school and beyond.

Oreos have more White friends than Black for obvious reasons. I have a lot of Black friends, but the relationships are mostly in passing at my church. The key to gaining respect is to have something to offer. I gain acceptance by my ability to help people overcome illness the doctors can't fix. Natural healing is one of my passions. I can quickly diagnose popular problems, and I suggest natural remedies that will make them better.

Fellow Oreos! Based on my research and lifelong learning, you must work hard to keep a perfect balance between Black and White cultures. We can never be our true selves in public, yet we can't hide from others who we really are. We are the outcasts of cultural norms, and we're kind of proud of that! Why not enjoy the best of both worlds, at least in your own mind? Go ahead and use the word "aks!" You will feel so much better letting key words go.

So many words so little time! Nobody knows the trouble we seen. I think you must be down for the cause to sing Negro spirituals, so I will leave that to the professionals. As much as we try to fit into our genetic Black communities, it's almost impossible for us to get true street creds from the school of hard knocks and ghettology. Besides, there's no place that will accept street credits so they're not worth anything anyway.

Help! I Need an Interpreter!

Talking to inner city Blacks is nearly impossible for me. It's hard for me to understand what people are saying. The accents, inflections, and the cussing do not come naturally for me! I'm not down for that, DAWG! I have Black friends who I really can't understand fully when they talk. Even when I text them, I get lost trying to decipher shortened words and phrases. Sometimes I smile and nod yes when I don't have an interpreter with me. People put me down for speaking properly, but my question is this: If my talk is "proper," why don't they want to learn to speak that way, too? Proper to them must be a derogatory description of "talking White."

I totally get what the Whites are putting down because, of course, I speak the language without any effort. I have been to many foreign countries, and I speak a little French, Turkish, and Swahili; just enough, yet I struggle mightily with real Black people's vocabulary and vernacular. It's so unique; Blacks have their own dictionary. The *Urban Dictionary,* which I have already referenced, is a resource I often use to look up definitions of words

I don't have a clue about. If someone says they were "Jonesed" at the park or were put in the "trick bag," I must play along until I get the *Urban Dictionary* out and look up the words spoken to me so I can decipher the meaning. Why are there so many definitions for the words "I seek"? I must remember the sentence and try to apply into which definition fits, option 1, 2, or 3? What makes the most sense in the context of what was said? Okay, I'll go with number 1, and hope I'm right!

Real Blacks assume Oreos know the *Urban Dictionary* well; they must think it's stored in our heads, but nothing could be further from the "gosh dagitty" truth. My conclusion is that the *Urban Dictionary* was created for Whites, news media, and people not of color in general. If you must have a dictionary for your cultural language, then you may have a problem fitting into the mainstream.

Diversity

Most people don't realize the diversity that exists within the Oreo community, or any other culture, for that matter. Cultures are made up of people, and we all know the diverse nature of people. So, let's abolish this idea of any one group being the same, totally homogeneous, as it just is not true. Although some cultures are more collectivistic in nature than others, they are still made up of individuals. Part of the real solution to embracing diversity rather than divisiveness is to understand the reality that even though we may belong to a group, we still have our individual thoughts, beliefs, ideas, ambitions, etc.

Think of the culture of over-the-road (OTR) 18-wheel truck drivers as an analogy. They all may live in the same world of long hauls, truck stop layovers, etc., however, there is still diversity, as each driver is an individual FIRST! And no, they aren't all big, burly men who swear and have a plethora of tattoos. These are superficial identifiers used all too often to classify people. "If the glove doesn't fit, we must acquit," to paraphrase a well-known comment.

Getting back to the truck driver analogy, I must include an example that emphasizes my point. I recently met an 18-wheel truck driver that would shatter anyone's illusion of occupational sameness. Maybe SHE should be considered an outlier, I don't know, but she was a tiny thing, barely five feet tall, had no tattoos, did not swear, was a mother of four, canned her own foods, and was all about sustainability of resources! How's THAT for diversity?! I asked her if people were surprised to see her when she climbed out of her rig, and she replied most definitely! I think it's awesome that she dared enter what is considered a "man's world," and I respect her greatly for her choice. I believe respect for one another's uniqueness is the answer to problems that arise within diverse populations.

The inability or unwillingness of people to toss the "us" vs. "them" mentality blocks change. The way society thinks about being different is convoluted. Lip service is given to the idea of diversity, but to be different all too often translates into "something's wrong with you." Again, when will the insanity stop?!

Culture refers to the customs, beliefs, and behaviors associated with a group of people. Culture can refer to a unit as small as the nuclear family or as large as a region or country. In this book, culture refers to those customs, beliefs, and attitudes that are thought to be White or Black.

What is Black culture? This is a question I once asked a college professor, and I don't know that I got a real straight answer. I will tell you this: Just because you are Black does not mean you fit in with Black culture, believe me, I know from first-hand experience.

Consider a fictional character named Bobby Lee Rayford, who was raised in a small village by a White family in rural Utah. Having Black skin in no way gives him a pass into Black culture. Bobby Lee is a full-fledged, certified, and stamped Oreo like me. Unless he adjusts better than I did, he will encounter many struggles trying to fit in somewhere. To many Whites, though, he must be part of Black culture because, after all, his skin is Black.

Discrimination and oppression directed toward Blacks is part of our cultural heritage, and we have learned behaviors in an attempt to be more acceptable to mainstream society. This has been necessary for our very survival, seriously. My wife grew up in the 1980s in a small town in the eastern Ohio Valley near the West Virginia border. On some weekends, the KKK would burn crosses in people's yards and harass Blacks on the edge of town. These events were terrifying, and there was no help from law enforcement, as some KKK members WERE law enforcement personnel and leaders in the community.

My parents, Floyd and Pearl White, grew up in the same region of Ohio in the 1950s, thus they experienced more racism than I could ever imagine in their community of hard-working coal miners and steel mill workers.

Rampant discrimination and oppression were part of White culture at the time, and although it may not be as blatant today, such behavior remains, and Oreos are not immune to being recipients. We have no secret "get out of jail" card, particularly when it comes to law enforcement. Most of us take extra precautions when interacting with law enforcement; learning how to deal with the police and other authority figures is part of our cultural upbringing.

On the positive side (at least I think it is positive), such situations make it easy to stand strong with RBP on fighting discrimination and other issues that really matter. Such "universal causes" bring us together, and for us Oreos, we try to take it a step further and encourage living respectfully and peacefully with everyone, Black,

White, whatever designated color you might be. It is greatly disturbing to me to be in the presence of Black people when they start talking smack about Whites. Oreos don't want to hear such things, as we identify a lot with White culture (as I have already stated more than once).

It's easier to gain acceptance in a culture when you have something to offer. For me, it's offering knowledge of natural healing, something for which I have a real passion. Many people come to me for help in overcoming illnesses when the traditional doctor's treatment has not helped. There are a lot of natural remedies out there that are effective, and these are what I recommend. Let me be clear, I am NOT a doctor, nor do I profess to be, I just have this "gift," so I use it. I also gain acceptance by being very accommodating and, unlike in Black culture, where a smile may be misconstrued as weakness, this is not so in White culture, so I smile a lot; I hope it doesn't look too goofy!

Fellow Oreos listen up! Based on my research and life-long learning, you must work hard to keep a balance between Black and White cultures. We can never be our true selves in public, and we probably will never gain any street creds from the school of hard knocks, but hey, street cred ain't all it's cracked up to be!

OREO-OLOGY VOL. IV

Oreology

O f course, this is a made-up term, and it means the study of Oreos. I'm going to put my old college training to work here and attempt to elaborate on the psychology behind this whole Oreo thing.

I often wonder how I would have turned out had I been raised "in the hood," or at least in predominantly Black neighborhoods. How would I be different had I not been a "military brat?" Seriously, I think about my hair being perfectly groomed, although hair is not something I have to deal with much today! Might I have been able to pull off awe-inspiring dance moves? Would I like sweet potato pie and urban music? One thing I DO know is that I absolutely draw the line when it comes to chitterlings. No way, no how, not EVER!! Don't get me wrong, I don't regret the opportunities I had growing up in a military family, it's just that I wonder if I missed out on what could have been.

I knew in high school that "ghetto neighborhoods" made me feel uneasy. My family attended an all-Black church for a few years back then, and although I found the "ghetto" neighborhood fascinating, I felt uneasy, as if I expected someone to pop out of nowhere to attack us at a traffic light. My White friends did not help any—they would talk about never going to certain parts of town because of the crime and shootings. I avoided interactions with Black males as much as possible because to me they seemed unpredictable, and I DID have some history of being the target of violence perpetrated by Black males in middle school. To some Blacks, I was a Black male in skin color only; it was their belief that I was programmed by "the Man."

Black females? I found them to be just as intimidating, just in a different way. I can safely say I have never met such demanding and straight-to-the-point females as they were. A common question was, "How much money do you make?" A common statement was, "Well, you look like you have a job." Lord have mercy! Perhaps these women were the minority, outliers, and I just happened to be unlucky enough to meet them.

Even today, grown man that I am, I can honestly say that I can't wait to get home from the church I currently attend. It is in an urban setting, and I have a lot of friends there. I feel safe among the people, but there is still the distant rumbling of disapproval, flashes in the distance, kind of like what you experience when a storm is approaching. What do I mean? Simply that the notion of "selling out" rears its ugly head once more. Some of my friends at the church say this is what I am doing by not living in an urban community, which includes the one in which my church is located. But these are places I would not want to be after dark. If I hear one more person ask me why I am living in a White neighborhood and why I don't live amongst my "brothers," I'm going to hyperventilate!

Of course, living in a White neighborhood also contributes to our angst because the Oreo is never good enough for either Whites or Blacks. Unless you can assimilate better than I have, there will be criticism from both groups; not only for what you are, but also for what you are not! It's crazy. We truly are like a sandwich, with us being the middle, and we all know what happens with things that are in the middle—they get squashed!! We are squeezed out by rejection, and this rejection of Oreos in social settings is a serious problem. The battle leaves psychological scars that I think are deeper than we realize. How then does an Oreo survive in such a dichotomous world where so few people accept us for who we are? You'll find my answer to that question in the next chapter.

Trust NoOne

Trust requires a certain comfort level, a belief that you are safe. Since Oreos find so few people who are accepting, we choose to trust no one. Isn't this how it goes in the animal kingdom? If we lived in that kingdom, would we be eliminated by natural selection? Would we be pushed out of the group, like what happened in the story of *The Ugly Duckling*? Perhaps so if we naively trust our environment. I cope with this by being ultra-observant, always on the alert for what "mode" I need to be in when I'm out in public. This daily stress wears me down. Now, when I am traveling abroad, I don't encounter the same things I do when in the U.S. When traveling, I am just another Black person, I am NOT an Oreo, and I don't strive to be White when abroad. Sad to say, it is easier for me to be myself when I am in a different country. How refreshing it is to not have to try to play both sides!

One thing I CAN trust is that I won't be accepted. RBP are open and honest to Oreos, but not in a nice way. I already talked about the criticism we experience, and I haven't yet figured out the reason for much of the criticism. Whites are a bit different in that their criticism is usually a bit more subtle, and I tend to be more comfortable talking with Whites, so conversations can be more expansive. In fact, the more I talk with someone the safer I generally feel, and my confidence and comfort level increases. I use humor a lot to try to break the ice and get people to be more open with me.

Expectations

Think about how you've been downgraded by people because of their expectations of how you should be, how you should look, how you should act, etc. Now, I realize this is not an experience exclusive to Oreos; I can only relate my own experiences and expound on my observations. Nobody knows the trouble us Oreos have seen, and that's as far as I will go with the Negro spirituals; I will leave the rest to the professionals. What? You expect me to be able to pull it off because I am Black? Nah! I can't even say I was exposed to this style of music growing up. I listened to the likes of Al Stewart, Barry Manilow (oh, how I LOVE to listen to Barry Manilow), The Beatles, Foreigner, Journey, the Carpenters, and others.

I am not the only Oreo who likes such music. In fact, I had a friend in high school who also was an Oreo who happened to be a fellow member of the marching band; he was also a huge Foreigner fan. Often during practice, he would play the solo from to "Urgent!" What a blast; that song ROCKS!! Yet the expectation remains, especially, I think, in the White community, that Blacks or

Oreos don't like that kind of music. I've even been asked by my White friends if I remember the "Slow Jamz." I hadn't a clue to what they were referring! It might be safe enough to tell my White friends what kind of music I truly like, but I don't dare let my Black friends know; I will let them rest in their expectation that I like what they do. By the way, according to them, I supposedly missed out on a lot of good songs. I disagree; however, I am just now discovering '80s R&B music, and I have to say I like it! There are so many different genres of music out there, we should not be expected to keep our taste in music confined to just a few.

Another expectation we might encounter concerns our preferred mode of communication which, according to White people, is supposed to consist of the use of slang, jibe, Ebonics, and Advanced Quantum Ebonics (AQE), which is so advanced that nobody knows what you're saying without an interpreter. We Oreos just don't roll that way. We are often clueless about this style of communication and about what is being said. For example, I tried to have a conversation with an older friend at church and I didn't get half of what he was saying. I smiled and laughed when he did, and thought to myself, "He must have a PhD in AQE!"

Then there are the expectations regarding athletics, singing, and dance. We are thought to be superior in these domains, but for me, not so much! When I was in high school and my friends saw me in a pair of shorts and running shoes, my abilities were elevated in their minds to Olympic status! In gym class, when we were lined up, some would say, "Oh, you're going to beat me," and I believed it! Imagine the disappointment when I, the hands-on favorite, lost the 100-yard dash to an "average" White person. I was totally embarrassed and felt ashamed because I believed that I had let down the Black side of Oreo cookie-ness. Dancing? Forget that right now. Singing? Not a chance! Even though my White friends thought I had moves like Michael Jackson (MJ) and a voice like him, too, I knew better and never attempted to showcase my rhythm deficiencies in public. There wouldn't be enough rhythm fuel in a caffeine laden IV drip to get me to do anything on beat! The same can't be said about my ability to PLAY music. I played well enough to earn a place in the Ohio State University Marching Band in the spring of 1989. O-H-I-O!!

Oreos don't live up to expectations from the Black community at all, and I will not lie, the resulting judgment hurts. Perhaps because we aren't "down for the cause," RBP's feel totally justified in treating us badly. Do they not realize that not everyone on planet Earth grew up the same way, with the same values and ideals? We are expected to adhere to all things Black, and our feet are held to the fire in a way that is very oppressive. Why do they continue to want us to be just like them? Why can't we be respected for our individuality? Ah, the age-old question.

Still, we Oreos do the best we can in order to try to meet expectations. When I meet Black strangers in public, I give the ubiquitous "'sup" head nod. It's absurd, but I feel like I'm a deep undercover secret agent. In these situations, I rarely smile, as this often is perceived as weakness. At the most, I might give half a smile, especially in the presence of a mixed crowd, meaning when females are present.

I'm going to expound on a story in the next chapter about assumptions and expectations made based on my voice alone, but I want to talk a little bit about that here as it fits so well with the topic. People make assumptions all the time that Black people "different." I can't tell you how many times I have been told, "You don't sound Black." Now, I don't take offense, but some Blacks do. My wife's voice is similar in that it does not "give away" her ethnicity. Both of us have fooled many people. Besides my voice, my last name is "White," so you can imagine the incredulity I get sometimes when meeting people sight unseen. People say with a rise in their voice, "Are you Kevin?" I would like to say I don't create the same expectations in my mind based on the sound of someone's voice and other characteristics, but you will read in the next chapter that this not the case, and that shame is on me.

Anyway, back to the sound of my voice and first meet. I can physically see the other person struggling to reconcile who they thought I was and who is standing before them. I think it is hilarious, and I get a good "internal" laugh out of it!

A Funny Thing Happened on the Way to Buying a PDA

Once I arranged to buy a PDA (personal digital assistant) from a woman on Craigslist who lived in DC. PDA? I'm really dating myself, right? Anyway, I was driving from Ohio to Virginia for a work conference, so it was on my way. Perfect!

I called her the day before I left. She sounded like a nice enough older White woman. We arranged to meet at a Starbucks kiosk at the Fair Oaks Mall at 2:00 p.m. on a Sunday afternoon. I explained to her what I was wearing so she could identify me. She described to me that she was wearing a purple striped shirt. Easy enough task, am I right? I ended up getting to the mall 15 minutes early, found my way to the kiosk, had a seat and waited… and waited… and waited for her to show. I thought I had wasted my time driving 480 miles to meet with no one.

After a while, I called the woman to see where she was. The phone of the Black woman sitting with her boyfriend on the bench next to me started ringing, and she answered her phone! I looked at her and said, "You're Amanda?" She replied with a startled look "Kevin?" We busted out laughing because she was looking for a White male and I was looking for a White female.

We had judged each other by voice alone; we stereo-typed what we would be looking for. In this case, we thought we knew beyond a doubt that the other was of the Caucasian persuasion. Even though we were wearing what we said we were for recognition, I purposely dismissed everyone that wasn't White, and apparently she and her boyfriend did the same to me. The kicker was we were sitting right next to each other for 15 minutes before we let go of our stereotypes based on our convoluted assumptions.

As expressed above, a neat superpower I possess is that I sound just like a Caucasian; my wife is the same way, too. We have both surprised many a caller when showing up in person after speaking on the phone. People do ask me if I am Kevin, which is pretty much normal, but there are some that are very, very, very surprised when I say that yes, I am. They can't believe that I'm the one they spoke with on the phone just a few minutes ago, "Are you Mr. White?" Obviously not what they expected. I almost feel disappointed I'm not living up to their idea of the guy on the other end of the phone line. I can see by their body language the adjustment they must make to move past that realization. I think it's hilarious!

This was the case when a new employee I hired was to stop by my house after several weeks of discussing the job, you guessed it, the phone. I gave him the address and told him I'd be out front, but when he pulled up there was a Black man on the phone in the front yard. He was about to drive past me until he saw me waving at him. Months later, he said to me, "Gee, I thought you were a White person. I wasn't sure who the Black guy was in front of your house until you started waving."

Maybe my last name, White, contributes to the idea that I am White? Is it my lack of "Black" words and phrases that fools people? This is what I mean by assumptions. People assume the stereotypes apply to every person in the group; everyone does this no matter what color they are. If you cannot pick up a clue over the phone, are you at a loss? How many of us try to imagine what the people on the phone looks like so we can judge them properly? It reminds me of Facebook, and how people troll the profile pages of those they argue with to find a weakness to exploit. It's all weird if you ask me.

Judging a Book by its Color...
Oops! I Mean Cover

I magine this scenario: Big box store, White customer: "Hi, I would like to see the latest Florida Georgia Line CD. Do you have it?" Store clerk: "Let me check the warehouse, kind sir. I will be back in a jiffy."

What happens when you ask a similar question, Oreos? The same clerk to a Black customer: "Excuse me store clerk, but do you have *The Best of Air Supply*? Store clerk: Hey, man! Let me check that for you. Notice they will add a bounce in their step to make you think they are down with Blacks. Nothing pulls my chain more than someone who does that to me just because I am a Black person. In their eyes, were all the same.

The clerk has to be thinking, well, my customer is Black, so I will act according to their people's behavior. They really like when I conversate with them like this: "Hey man! What's up? How can I help you?" Really?! What's an Oreo to do? This is awkward to us because at this point the White clerk is speaking Blacker than we can respond on our own. We can't throw down like that! How does he know that lingo better than I do? Have I failed the Black race? I need to brush up on my Black flow again.

The double standard here is that Oreos are expected to be able to talk like real Blacks based on their race traits. However, all Whites need to do is add the word "man" to every sentence and the real Blacks are good with that. Seriously, why can't we all be treated the same?

In school, they tell you never to judge a book by its cover, but never say not to judge a person by his skin color. Maybe that should be added to the curriculum, I'm just saying. The perceived ideal of the Black person you see in me is just as foreign to me as he is to you. Treat me as a customer, not as a Black or White man. Don't follow me while I'm in there. Yeah, I used to work retail, so I know your tactics.

The only time I received instant respect as an Oreo in a public situation was when I was in my military uniform. People recognized me as a military person first, so I was free of being a stereotyped Black person. I was respected and thanked for my service by strangers. Even in small towns and Black communities, people seemed to trade their Black assumptions for military ones. Trust me, it's better to be seen and respected as a soldier than a Black man any day. That respect, honor, and recognition does not exist among strangers as an unknown-quantity Black man.

I used to work in the hardware department at the Anderson's general store when I was going to college. One night I got off work at 11:00 p.m., and on my way home I was followed and then stopped by the Reynoldsburg, Ohio, police for no apparent reason. Oh shucks, I know how to act for the police, no problem. Here I go with the smile and polite conversation again. I asked what the problem was, and the police officers had no answer. I thought to myself, why can't they see I am one of them, down for the other cause?

They made up a story that a retail store was robbed at 11:00, and that my car matched the description of the getaway car. I replied that I had just left a retail store, and that I wanted to know which one it was because I was truly concerned. They gave me a hard time, and told me if I kept talking, I'd be going downtown with them.

I couldn't believe this was happening to me, an Oreo who never broke the law, a military member who respected law enforcement. They looked at my driver's license and ran my plates for what seemed like 20 minutes. You know how embarrassing it is to be pulled over; imagine being Black and being pulled over in a

White community. After a while they finally let me go, but I lost a lot of faith in Reynoldsburg law enforcement that night.

I had heard stories of Blacks being pulled over for no reason, but never thought those stories applied to Oreos. After it happened, I remembered what my father used to say to me about how it wasn't easy being a Black person in this world. My father grew up in a small country town call Cadiz, Ohio, in the 1950s, and his perspective was grounded in the reality of that time. But you know, it was still relevant that day I was stopped. On another date, in a park close to our house, Dad and I walked our dog and were stopped by a policeman who asked what we were doing in that neighborhood. He gave Dad a hard time and didn't believe his explanation at first. It happened to be the neighborhood park where we lived! My whole Oreo world was falling apart, and I couldn't fix it.

I have read in a few books by Walter Mosely that, during the '60s, Black men were taken downtown to a police station to be beaten up by corrupt officers; 1986 was not so very far from when that happened. This wasn't the world I knew as a military brat. Reality was setting in with a vengeance.

First the people are corrupt and now the public police? This was another situation where my smiles and respect profited me nothing. The police officers only saw our skin color and judged us before they got the facts. Both incidents happened in White neighborhoods where very few Blacks lived, and we were part of the community. The bottom line is, Oreo or not, you are Black first and foremost. You have no power in some situations that come to you.

In the '70s and early '80s, when a bogus police stop was made by officers who thought you were up to no good in a White neighborhood, you had to really pull the proverbial rabbit out of your magic hat to help keep things from escalating. I had one get out of jail card that I didn't bring up with the Reynoldsburg police that maybe I should have: My military ID had gotten me respect from the police at other times, but that night I was so upset that I couldn't think straight.

Have you ever been the only Black person in the room and people treat you like you from the straight hood? At that point, you're the one everyone else is trying to figure out how to not offend, deal, speak, approach, etc., etc. Why? Because you're "different" in a lot of their minds. Now, I'm certainly not saying everyone sees us this way, but you know what I mean.

Dismissing social extremes and staying inside of our normal circles, we see ourselves as being equally "White" and can hang with anyone in the room. It's like being the boy who was raised by wolves. We know we aren't really wolves, yet on a subconscious we think we are. Even though we grow up knowing were obviously not White, we choose to not make it an issue. Our social and mental states of mind always outweigh our physical reality.

Real Blacks and Whites have comfort in their own worlds, whereas the Oreo has no comfort but among his or her own kind. What do I mean? Whites are more comfortable with other Whites in their social and economic class. The same truth holds with Blacks among other Blacks in the same categories. Whites can identify with cultural norms and ease into the comfort of interacting with other "White wolves" virtually unnoticed. Blacks can share dens with other "Black wolves" because we're all social animals. Add in one different race, even of the same cultural norms and socioeconomic class, and voila! Everything changes. Why? Didn't I explain that already? Pay attention, please.

Oreos like to imitate their Black counterparts by pretending to be what they are not to each other. We say things like, "Yo dawg, wassup?" "We fin to roll to da club!" "Fo real?" "Yeah Bro!" The key is to shorten some words. But wait: Dawg is longer than dog. Some words are combined: What's + up = wassup. Leave the letter "R" off other words: for = fo. Real Black talk is a whole other language you would have to be exposed to, and

I'm sure I am doing no justice to these phrases. I envy the talk and would like to be able to flow like that, but when I do get a phrase down, I can't keep it straight, and it doesn't sound right. I stay in my lane and talk the White suburban dialect. You know, the one I get criticized and ridiculed for.

Green with Envy

I wonder how many Oreos are envious of the Black and White races. In this oversimplified world, everything is Black and White. Blacks and Whites have solid identities; everything is cut and dry. If you're White you know your culture, and the same for Blacks. Oreos don't even know who other Oreos are. I'm not about to ask someone in my neighborhood if they're an Oreo. How do you even find friends or know if your current friends are Oreos? Someone who was a military brat for most of their youth is often a prime suspect that I can relate to.

For me, outside of that small pool of people it is impossible to know. Fortunately, I know many people who grew up that way and joined the military themselves. When you're born in a military hospital, go to military schools, and think everyone in the world is in the military, chances are you want to join, too. It may have been the only life you knew. For me it was the only life I understood and loved.

I would prefer to just be me and not labeled an Oreo. If people would accept each other as they are, we wouldn't have to worry about what others think of our outward behavior. It's a crazy society when people question whether your Black identity is authentic or not. Why would anyone really want to worry that much about others they have nothing to do with? Why would someone take time to even care if I talk different than they expect me to? Do people have that much time on their hands to probe into other people's lives?

Oreos are closer to Whites, but their skin color gets in the way of achieving equality they think they have. If Whites judge Blacks by any standard other than their own, then that would include every Oreo under the sun. You can work with someone for years and never know what they really think about an Oreo until a situation brings out a stereotypical comment.

One of an Oreo's superpowers is invisibility to Whites. To Whites, Oreos and Blacks are synonymous. No difference can exist between the two because they don't know who an undercover Oreo might be unless the Oreo tells them. Still, I'm not sure the Whites care or understand what that means anyway.

Fitting In

Oreos, do you find yourself trying to prove to Whites you don't know that you are more like them? You know, safe, and, um, how should I say this, mild, meek, and acceptable? I am talking about an initial meeting in public or among people with whom you are introduced. What we're trying to communicate is, "I'm not Black like you think, I'm like one of you guys, you know, good." Really! See how I am acting and speaking? Yeah, I'm swell, too. Please ignore the color of my skin and we will get along swimmingly! In these situations, you're pathetically overemphasizing your normal behavior, and you do it to try to dispel presumed notions. You want to make sure the expectation of you being Black does not equal trouble or paint you as someone to fear. You so want approval from this population group with whom you believe you identify more. You want to fit in somewhere. My approach works sometimes and sometimes it doesn't.

There are those who go to what I think are extremes to try to fit in. I am talking about racial "passing," where a Black person is so light-skinned that he or she visually appears to be White. There is a film called *Across the Tracks* that documents two Black sisters in 1960s Georgia, one quite light and the other dark. The light-toned sister decides to pass for White, which sets off a 40-year period of growing animosity between the two. I highly suggest you put this film on your list as a must-see, and thus I am not going to give away any more of the story line.

When my family moved into a home in a White neighborhood in Columbus, Ohio, in 1980, our neighbors took notice. My brother Mark and I went on an "Oreo Peace Tour," and set out to meet and greet all our neighbors. We used our smiles and our "acceptable" behavior (meek, etc.) to eliminate the notion that we were like the Black students we had encountered at Johnston Park Middle School. We were determined to fit in with the rest of our neighbors, and our efforts were rewarded! Yay! We made it clear that we weren't people to fear, a concept that we never encountered while living on base. We were all about the Oreo cause of inclusion, acceptance, and harmony.

When I married my wife, Carolyn, I was assigned to a military base in Swanton, Ohio, an area outside of Toledo. We were looking for temporary housing as Toledo was too urban for us. We desired a mixed community, and we were told by one of my co-workers that there were Blacks living in the nearby town of Swanton. It turned out that Swanton was an all-White, not so Black, not so friendly village, and a month after we moved into our rental apartment, people started moving out in droves. I kid you not! Welcome to Swanton—NOT! No one bothered us, but there was the assumption that we were not good for property values and probably were unsafe to be around their children. No one wanted to talk to us; only at work was there any degree of acceptance. We couldn't wait for our lease to expire.

I don't test the whole issue of fitting in and being accepted when cruising through small towns. When I don't see any Black people, I wonder if it is even safe for me to stop anywhere, even along a main road. Knowing there are other Blacks in town provides me with a certain comfort level. It tells me the water is safe, and I can go ahead and take a dip.

Would Caucasians feel the same degree of not fitting in should they find themselves in an all-Black neighborhood? Would it not cause the same degree of concern? Possibly, but I believe it would be safer for them to move to small town that is predominantly Black than vice versa. There is an environment where Oreos feel the safest and that is good old suburbia, USA. After all, isn't that where Oreos are born and raised?

This issue of fitting in is not limited to Whites, as evidenced by what I have written, but I want to comment just a bit further. It seems to me that RBP not only shut us out, but that they would like to eradicate us Oreos altogether. Are we that much of a cancer to them? There seems to be fear that we are might grow and spread. The more I think about it, I wonder if that might be the reason I so often get the cold shoulder when I do my best to fit in. It's very disheartening when other Blacks treat you like a joke or worse. I consider some of the behavior that has been directed towards me to be a personal attack. What is even more distressing is that when a White person tries to "act Black," they are more readily accepted. They are not held to the same standard, and somehow their efforts are okay and tolerated while mine aren't. Why? I believe a large part of it is that the "jive" White person's efforts to fit in are considered harmless and kind of sweet. The Oreo, however, is viewed as a traitor. These attitudes and resultant behaviors are truly enough to move me to tears.

To RBP, us Oreos are lowest on the totem pole, beneath those who are biracial. Biracial people have one parent who is White. Not all biracial people are Oreos, but I would say most Oreos have a biracial background as it would be more likely that they would live in White society. It just depends. I had a discussion with a biracial friend who insisted that being biracial made them an Oreo by default. I did not totally agree with this, but I capitulated some. The quintessential factor is the culture in which a person is raised.

Trust me on this. I'm not saying that biracial people have it exactly easy, as White people generally label biracial people as Black, and therefore not their equal. But Whites don't ridicule biracial people as mercilessly as they do Oreos. Biracial people seem to be more of a new class of Blacks in America, an identity that fits into the stratification paradigm. At least they have a place to fit and their identity is generally understood; us Oreos, nope!

Interestingly, I would say most Blacks are familiar with the term Oreo as it applies to humanity, but I find that most Whites have never heard the term. An Oreo to them is of the cookie variety, period! Does that mean most Whites don't differentiate Blacks or does it mean most Blacks do?

Shallow Anyone?

A s I mentioned previously, humans always note physical differences between other people or groups. If it's not skin color, it's weight, age, hair color, or religion, just to name a few.

One example of physical discrimination is toward overweight people. The governor of New Jersey, Chris Christie, is a rather larger person. What's the first thing people use to degrade and put him down? His weight! He's been called Chris Twinkie, Big Boy, puffer fish and more. No matter what he does or believes in, we humans see him as fat without a ph. The way he can shed this problem is by eliminating the target. Yep, the only way he can escape this is to lose the weight so he can look "normal." That's just what he did for a while, but apparently, he stopped caring what people thought of him.

Conversely, there is no real solution for the physical race of a person. New Jersey Senator Cory Booker cannot do anything to counteract his physical difference. No matter how much he accomplishes or makes an impact, he will always be a Black senator with a racial "handicap" he can never change. He was born with it, and he will die with it. Someday they will have race changes, or do they already?

Physically identifying as a particular race is not a bad thing, but it is a factor between fitting in and standing out. In some situations, however, race can be an advantage. I'm sure our wise politicians take advantage of that when they can. Speaking to urban audiences, a Black politician has a great advantage over unlike competition. But here is the ironic part of the politics: Blacks will support the most Oreo of their political leaders. WHAT?! WAIT!!

President Obama appeared to be a straight up Oreo to the nth degree, yet he got nothing but respect from the Black community. How can this be? He was one of us!!! Do I have to run for office to get respect? Why? Because his parents were White and Black, so his biracial make-up made him acceptable?

This brings back the earlier point that biracial people are more Black than White. Is this another form of discrimination? We always call President Obama Black when he was only half Black. We've never had a real Black president! We've had a Blacker one. According to Black Oreo-haters, you're never a real Black unless you act Black, too. To the Whites, if you look like you're Black you are 100% Black.

President Obama got a lot of credit from Blacks, but he did not really do anything for us that was tangible. President Trump, however unpopular he is with many Blacks, has created a record economy with many opportunity zones and tax cuts for all Americans, including Blacks. Yet he gets no credit from us. I am sure our fictional character Bobby Lee and probably most Oreos as a group have a different opinion on this.

The Black vote in this country is largely monolithic, whereas Whites are more independent in that their vote can go either way. You won't find many independent and undecided Blacks in your election polls. We Blacks always get assumptions about the way we vote. Again, Blacks cannot be individual thinkers even if they are Oreos. If Blacks keep voting the same way, their voting assumptions will continue to push the oneness narrative. But wait! Oreos aren't Black in the eyes of RBP's! Like Whites, they could go either way in the voting booth.

What If?

W hat if there was an Oreo gated community in every city? Would they be located between the Black and White neighborhoods?
You know, in the middle, like the Oreo cookie? There
could be Oreo churches, restaurants, and schools. Ah,
I can see it now, "Uncle Tom High School, home of
the Fighting Coconuts!" Our school colors will be black
and white (technically, those aren't colors at all, they are
called neutrals, but we all know Black is anything but
neutral in the human being world). Of course, all the
citizens would have to be certified and interviewed to
be accepted to any Oreo gated community.

We could even have an affirmative action program to
diversify our student body and staff. Taking it further,
what if we had our very own state allowing us to live
totally worry-free? Imagine an all-Oreo government,
police force, fire department, and mushroom and latte
committee. Whites love their mushrooms and lattes…
with milk!

In Oreo City, it would be difficult to "spin" a crime story to fit an agenda. Suppose a citizen was gunned down

by law enforcement, the Oreo media would report it as a tragedy concerning a citizen in Oreo City, while the Black and White media representatives would call it a racial hate crime before they learned the facts. The facts? Both officers were quasi-Black, Oreo-certified.

In Oreo society, would stereotypes disappear? Probably not, because there may be degrees of Oreo-ness among the Oreo people, which would allow for labeling and classifying, which leads to stratification, kind of like how it is now with varying degrees of skin color. There's light Black, medium Black, dark Black, and the blackest of Black. An Oreo society, in theory, would be the perfect balance between both Black and White races. Black on the Outside and White on the Inside, or BOWI. This acronym sounds like a native culture somewhere, doesn't it?

If people are people, they will differentiate and stratify themselves to gain advantage over others. If you don't believe this, look up the word colorism and you will see that among some Caribbean islands, the elite are made up of lighter-skinned citizens, while darker people tend to be just part of the general population. I noticed this interesting phenomenon when I visited the Bahamas a few years back. I noticed the entertainment and working class were all darker-skinned, while the lighter-skinned citizens had an air of upward mobility. Colorism is a racial issue on many islands; the darker you are, the less you are revered. And the same goes for the United States; historically, the lighter-skinned a person, the better their chance for success and greater social status. As the old saying goes, "If you're White, you're right/If you're yellow, you're mellow/If you're brown, stick around/If you're Black, get back." Do you see how the very dark are at the bottom? It seems primitive, doesn't it? Perhaps humans are forever primitive in nature, and there's no way to escape it. Does it remind you of your home country?

What if this color stratification did not exist? Skin color would not equal good or bad, desirable or undesirable. Dark-skinned people would be promoted in the media just as much as light-skinned people. People would not have to feel like they had to bleach their skin to escape further discrimination. Oreos would not exist either, except in cookie form! Merit and ability would be the criteria for advancement and status. There would be an end to all this shallow pettiness.

What if Oreos could wear a unique device that makes others aware that they identify with other Whites? This could offer reassurance to those who jump to conclusions, prematurely deciding that the Oreo fit the typecast of the RBP. We could call it the "Pass 4" device, and they could be worn while out in public. People with the "Pass 4" could ride around any town without impunity and purchase items from any chicken restaurant guilt-free. However, this device would come with a caveat: An Oreo is not to wear it around other Blacks as they may very well use it against the person, taunting that person mercilessly. Warning!! Your "Pass 4" device must always be secured when not in use. If an RBP with evil intentions ever got ahold of one, he or she could destroy the Oreo's reputation by posing as a wolf in sheep's clothing.

Alas, for now we are forced to abandon anything stereotypically considered "Black" and enjoy such luxuries in the closet. These luxuries are caustic out in the real world. For now, the "What If"scenario is an exercise in futility. I have little faith that there will ever be a time when we all get along. Full integration does not work—that has already been tried. I only brought up the ridiculousness of the Oreo gated city to prove a point. The point is that not everyone can't get along, no matter how homogenous they are; we are just primal beings with technology. Remember, I said it here first.

Conclusion

I t's evident that everyone judges whether they realize it or not. It is the nature of humankind to differentiate, using whatever measure leads to the greatest advantage. The evidence in this book is somewhat compelling.

The Oreo dilemma stems from intolerance from Whites AND Blacks. Oreos are in an awkward position, trying to identify with more than one group only to be subjected to criticism and ridicule. The gift in being an Oreo is having a more intimate understanding of Black AND White thought processes and the culture of each group. We are very aware of stereotypes and actions and how these are impacted by one's culture.

Oreos can bring both sides together, and I believe we are all ambassadors on a mission. That's the cause! There! I just justified the existence of Oreos. We are good for more than just confusing others. If given the opportunity, we can shed light on dark realities. This could be the whole purpose for us! We are the salt of the world! Nah! Rather, the salt and pepper packets of the world— ready to commingle and make whatever is being tasted just that more flavorful!

I hope my humor, personal experiences, and research have helped bring light to this complex reality. Light brings hope and awareness, which opens the possibility for change.

My name is Kevin. I am an African American trying to cultivate my own garden.